C B
MILK HA Kra
Krakow, Kari.
The Harvey Milk story
GIL 1071039414

SEP 1 5 2006

WITHDRAWN

WORN, SOILED, OBSOLETE

D0506845

The
HARVEY MILK
Story

By Kari Krakow

Illustrated by David Gardner

Two Lives Publishing

Published by
Two Lives Publishing
508 North Swarthmore Avenue
Ridley Park, PA 19078
www.TwoLives.com

Copyright © 2001 by Kari Krakow
Illustrations copyright © 2001 by David Gardner
Book production by Kids At Our House

All rights reserved. No part of this book may be reproduced or transmitted in
any form or by any means, electronic or mechanical, including photocopying,
recording, or by any information storage and retrieval system, without
the written permission of the Publisher, except where permitted by law.

ISBN: 0-9674468-3-X

Library of Congress Cataloging-in-Publication Data
2002100994

1 2 3 4 5 6 7 8 9 10

Printed in China

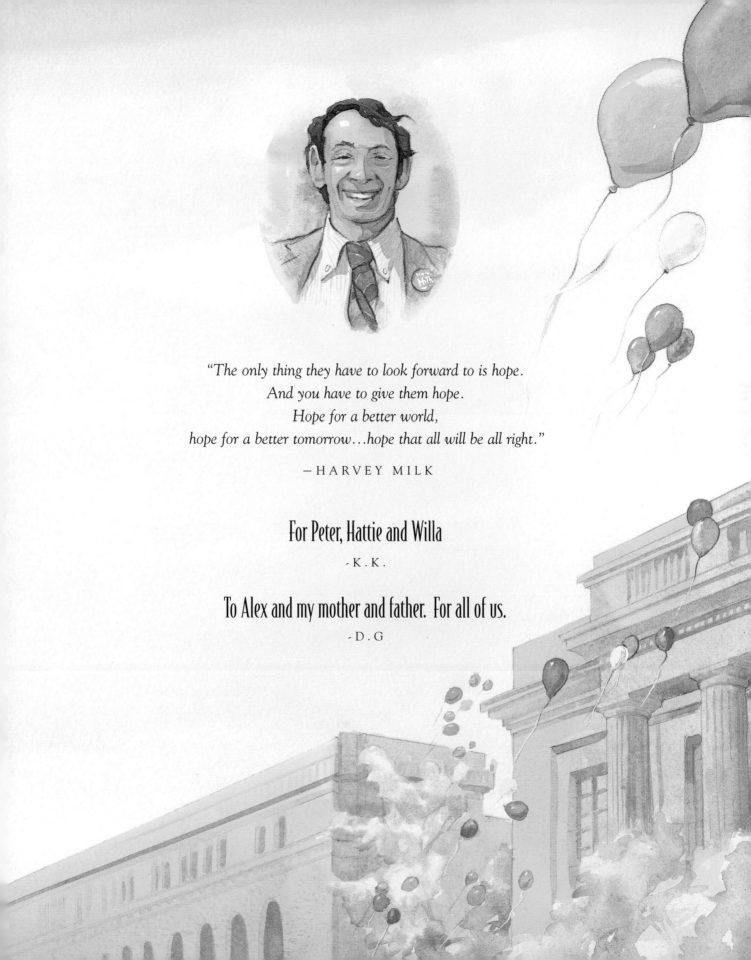

"The only thing they have to look forward to is hope.
And you have to give them hope.
Hope for a better world,
hope for a better tomorrow…hope that all will be all right."

— HARVEY MILK

For Peter, Hattie and Willa

- K.K.

To Alex and my mother and father. For all of us.

- D.G

No one would have ever guessed that the little kid with big ears would one day make history. Harvey Bernard Milk was born the second son of a middle class Jewish family on May 22nd, 1930. He grew up in Woodmere, New York.

As a child, Harvey loved to be the center of attention. On Saturday afternoons, he would delight his family by pretending to conduct the unseen orchestra blaring from the radio on the mantle.

Minnie Milk was especially proud of her intelligent and energetic son. She recognized in him an independent spirit and encouraged him to stand up for what he believed in. Harvey never forgot the day his mother told him about the brave Jews of the Warsaw Ghetto, who continued to defend themselves even when outnumbered and surrounded by Nazis.

Harvey loved sports. His height made him a natural on the basketball team, and he participated in track and wrestling. He also played linebacker for Bayshore High's football team wearing jersey number 60.

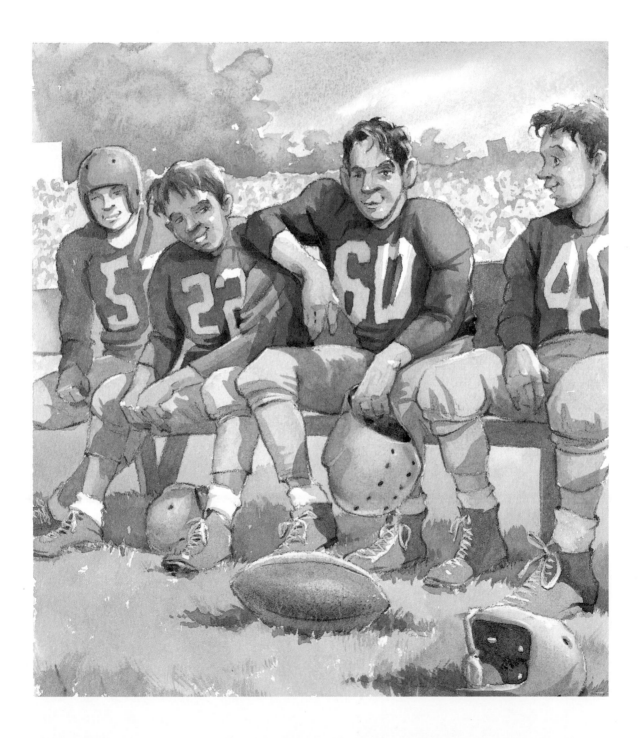

Harvey was always popular. It was hard to find anyone who wasn't his friend.
Always ready with a joke and a smile, he knew how to make
people laugh. He had something special that years later politicians would
call charisma. Everyone knew Harvey and liked him.

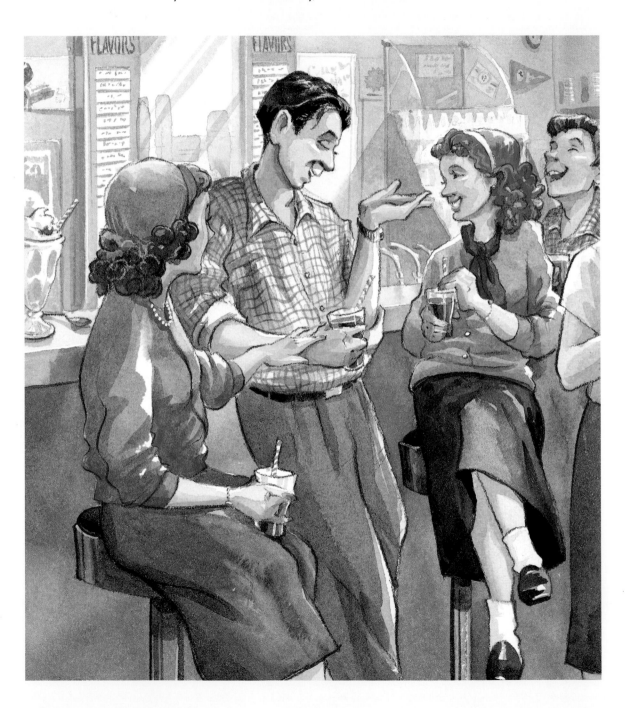

What his friends and family didn't know was that Harvey was growing up gay. Harvey knew he was gay by the time he was fourteen, but he would keep that part of himself a closely guarded secret for many years to come. Like so many people of his time, he was afraid of what would happen to him if others knew he was gay. Fears that he would be beaten up at school and abandoned by his friends and family troubled his sleep and tormented his days.

A good student, Harvey finished high school a year early and went on to Albany State Teachers College. He continued playing football and basketball and was the sports editor for *The State College News* in his senior year. Harvey was handed his college diploma on a warm day in June 1951, while his parents proudly looked on.

After college, Harvey joined the Navy. He became an expert deep-sea diver and taught others to maneuver heavy equipment on the ocean floor. Rising rapidly through the ranks, Harvey soon became chief petty officer on the *U.S.S. Kittiwake*, a submarine rescue vessel that cruised the Pacific. When he went to his brother Robert's wedding, he looked so handsome in his navy uniform that his family and friends all wondered when he would settle down and get married to the "right girl."

Harvey did fall in love and settle down. But the right person was a handsome young man named Joe Campbell. They moved together to Rego Park, New York, where Harvey taught math and science at Hewlitt High School and coached basketball after school. They were happy together, but Harvey kept their relationship a secret. Harvey feared he would lose his job, his friends and his family if people found out he was gay. Keeping such a big part of their lives secret put a lot of stress on Harvey and Joe's relationship, and after six years they separated.

Harvey was tired of hiding the fact that he was gay. So when he met and fell in love with Scott Smith, they moved together to a neighborhood in San Francisco known as the Castro. The Castro was becoming a gay neighborhood, a place where a gay couple could walk down the street, hold hands, and show all the signs of affection, joy and pride that people do when they are in love.

Harvey and Scott put their money together and invested in camera supplies and a five-year lease for a Victorian storefront on Castro Street. They moved in upstairs, and opened Castro Camera on the first floor. For the first time in his life, Harvey felt like he could finally be himself.

Harvey took time to talk to his customers, and he was always ready to help or offer advice. New Castro residents came by to ask where to look for an apartment or how to find that first job. The store's large picture windows displayed announcements, petitions and notices of neighborhood meetings. Castro Camera quickly became a community center.

As Harvey listened to people, he realized that the Castro community needed a leader. Gay people had no legal protection, and they risked losing their jobs and homes. They were harassed by the police. To help change laws and fight for the rights of gay people, Harvey decided to run for public office in San Francisco.

Many people wanted to help elect Harvey Milk. They liked him and his ideas. Friends, neighbors, and customers volunteered their time to send out mailings, paint posters, and answer phones. Eleven-year-old Medora Payne came every day after school to lick envelopes and hand out brochures for Harvey. She organized a fundraiser at her school, earning $39.28 for his campaign.

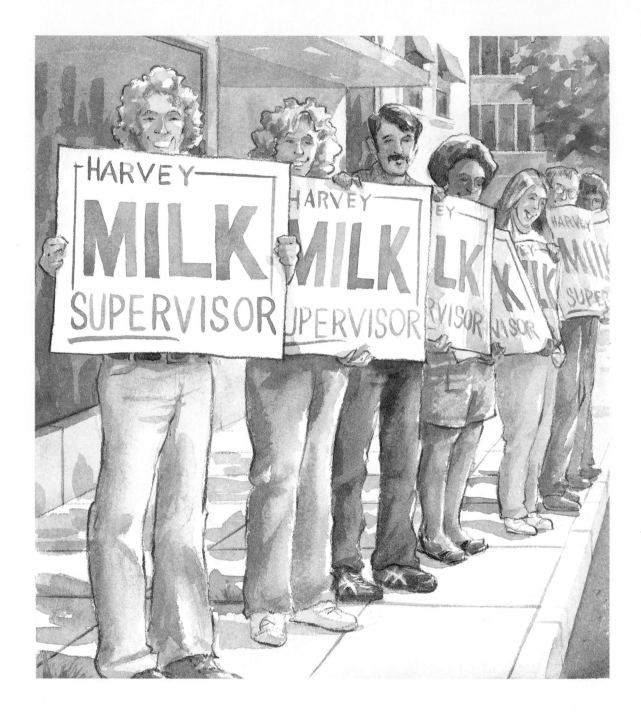

Some people thought that the Harvey Milk campaign was a joke. They thought it was impossible for an openly gay candidate to get elected, because none had before. Harvey ran for public office in San Francisco three times between 1973 and 1976. Each time he lost.

But Harvey didn't lose hope or give up. He knew that having an openly gay leader at City Hall would give people the courage to be proud of who they were. He kept on trying, and each time he ran for office he came closer to winning. He worked tirelessly talking to the people in his district. Harvey showed respect for the diverse cultures of his community. He spoke out for the rights of people who were often ignored by city government: African Americans, Asian Americans, senior citizens, people with disabilities, and gays and lesbians.

More and more people began to agree with his ideas about fairness and justice. They sensed that Harvey would stand up for what he believed in and make a difference in city government. In 1977, he ran again for San Francisco's Board of Supervisors, and this time he won. On a rainy day in January, on the steps of San Francisco's City Hall, Harvey Milk was sworn into office, the first openly gay elected city official in the United States of America. Harvey Milk had made history.

As a supervisor, Harvey Milk got to work on the issues that the people of San Francisco cared about: schools, parks, police protection and housing. He helped make laws to ensure the quality of life for all people. After fighting against the closing of a neighborhood school, he said, "Our cities must not be abandoned. They're worth fighting for, not just by those who live in them, but by industry, commerce, unions, everyone. What we need is a neighborhood where people can walk to work, raise their kids, enjoy life. That simple."

Supervisor Milk fought hard to introduce a gay rights bill for San Francisco. This law would protect gay people from discrimination at work and when choosing a home. Ten of the eleven supervisors on the city council voted for the gay rights bill, and San Francisco's Mayor, George Moscone, enthusiastically signed the bill into law. "I don't do this enough," said the Mayor, "taking swift and unambiguous action on a substantial move for civil rights."

The gay people of San Francisco were now legally protected from being harassed at their workplace and losing their jobs and homes. More and more gay people were able to come out of hiding and live in the open. In the 1978 Gay Freedom Day Parade, nearly 400,000 people marched through downtown San Francisco. Harvey Milk proudly rode at the center of the parade as thousands cheered.

That day Harvey Milk gave a speech to the huge mass of people that had settled in front of City Hall. He called for a Gay Rights March in Washington, D.C., to show the nation that gay people would no longer hide. Harvey Milk was a hero.

But some people felt threatened by the growing gay movement. They hated and feared the idea of gay people having the same rights as everyone else. Dan White was one of those people. He was the only supervisor to vote against the gay rights bill. He tried to prevent the San Francisco Gay Freedom Parade from taking place. He was voted down.

Dan White didn't like to lose. He was so frustrated by his lack of power and so jealous of Harvey Milk's growing popularity that he resigned from the Board of Supervisors. Ten days later, he changed his mind and asked to be reappointed. When Mayor Moscone would not give him his job back, he was angry.

On a gray November morning, Dan White crawled through a basement window at the back of City Hall with a loaded gun.

Dan White entered the mayor's office and, after a brief argument took place, shot Mayor George Moscone. Reloading his gun, he hurried down the hall to Harvey Milk's office. Five shots rang out.

Both Mayor Moscone and Harvey Milk were killed.

People everywhere were stunned by the news of the double assassination. They left their homes, jobs and schools to mourn the loss of these two great leaders. Crowds began forming in front of City Hall. By nightfall thousands filled the mile-long street that ran from the Castro to City Hall. They stood in silence, carrying candles. That night the people of San Francisco wept.

Harvey Milk was gone but his dream lived on. That next October, 1979, over one hundred thousand people responded to his call. They participated in the first Gay Rights March in Washington, D.C., and thousands carried portraits in memory of the slain leader. Harvey Milk would not be forgotten.

EPILOGUE

Harvey Milk's memory continues to live on in many places and in many ways. In San Francisco the Harvey Milk Memorial Plaza marks the entrance to the Castro, and the neighborhood elementary school that Harvey fought to keep open proudly bears his name, The Harvey Milk Civil Rights Academy.

Harvey Milk believed that one person could make a difference in the lives of others. His legacy continues to inspire and give people hope as they struggle for justice. Today there is an ever-increasing number of cities and states that have enacted civil rights protections for gay people. More and more openly gay people are running for office and getting elected. Harvey Milk once said: "The true function of politics is not just to pass laws, but to give hope." Harvey Milk pioneered a road to freedom. He showed the world that all people can have their hopes realized.

AUTHOR'S NOTES

Pg 3

"Harvey never forgot the day his mother told him about the brave Jews of the Warsaw Ghetto, who continued to defend themselves even when outnumbered and surroundedby Nazis."

Harvey Milk was inspired by the struggle of the brave Jews in the Warsaw Ghetto. In 1940 the Jewish residents of Warsaw, Poland were forced into a designated area of the city, which was sealed off by a ten-foot wall topped by barbed wire and guarded by Nazi troops.

Conditions in the ghetto were unbearable. Thousands of people died from starvation, disease and cold. In 1942, 300,000 Jews were deported to the city of Treblinka. When reports of mass killings in Treblinka leaked back to the ghetto, the surviving Jews organized a rebellion. They refused to report for deportation, and bravely battled the Nazis against incredible odds. After days of fighting, the Nazi troops retreated. Even though the Nazis later destroyed the ghetto, this struggle inspired resistance groups throughout Europe to fight against Nazi oppression.

For more information about the Warsaw Ghetto, contact the United States Holocaust Memorial Museum, http://www.ushmm.org/.

Pg. 5

"Like so many people of his time, he was afraid of what would happen to him if others knew he was gay."

Pg. 12

"Gay people had no legal protection, and they risked losing their jobs and homes. They were harassed by the police."

When Harvey Milk was a young man, discrimination against groups of people was commonplace. African American people were denied equal access to public places. Jewish people were barred from membership in clubs and organizations. Women were not allowed entry to many universities. Gay people were also the subject of prejudice and mistreatment. They could be harassed, arrested, and sometimes beaten by police for going to gay bars or clubs.

Violence against gays and lesbians was ignored by the law enforcement and legal systems. Gays and lesbians were routinely fired from their jobs and evicted from their homes. For these reasons, gay people were forced to hide their identities and relationships. Many people have fought to create laws that protect against discrimination. Harvey Milk was one of these people.

Today the fight continues. In the United States there are now 13 states with anti-discrimination laws that protect gay and lesbian people. Cities and towns across the country are adopting civil rights ordinances to help ensure that lesbians and gay men receive fair treatment.

For more information about laws protecting gay people, contact the Lambda Legal Defense Fund, http://www.lambdalegal.org/.

Pg. 12

"Fears that he would be beaten up at school and abandoned by his friends and family troubled his sleep and tormented his days."

When Harvey was young, gay people were forced to keep their lives a secret. They were misrepresented and misunderstood. Even friends and family members might reject someone if they found out he or she was gay. Harvey Milk gave many people the courage to live openly despite the risks.

Today most people know someone who is gay. More and more openly gay people are acknowledged for the important contributions they make to our society. Many people have thought about the possibility of a family member or friend being gay, but even today young gay people are harassed in school and rejected by their friends and family. Harvey Milk believed that one person could make a difference in the lives of others. Each of us, straight and gay, can make a difference too. We can respect and value the gay people in our lives and encourage our schools and communities to be safe and welcoming places for all.

For more information about creating supportive and welcoming school communities, contact GLSEN (Gay, Lesbian and Straight Education Network), http://www.glsen.org/.

For more information about supportive family and friends, contact PFLAG (Parents, Families and Friends of Lesbians and Gays), http://www.pflag.org/.

Acknowledgments

The author is indebted to Duane Diviney, John Oakley, June Locke, Kathleen Kesson, and Sarah Schulman for their kind assistance and encouragement in writing this book.

Bibliography

Books:
Marcus, Eric. Making History: The Struggle for Gay and Lesbian Equal Rights. New York: HarperCollins, 1992.
Miller, Neil. Out of the Past, Gay and Lesbian History from 1869 to the Present. New York: Vintage Books, 1995.
Shiltz, Randy. The Mayor of Castro Street: The Life and Times of Harvey Milk. New York: St. Martin's Press, 1982.

Films:
Epstein, Rob and Richard Schmiechen. "The Times of Harvey Milk." San Francisco: Black Sands Productions, 1984.
Stein, Peter. "The Castro." San Francisco: KQED, 1997.

Periodicals:
The Advocate 1977-1979.
The San Francisco Chronicle and Examiner 1977-1979.

1071039414